AUG -- 2017

W9-BYK-176

DISCARD

BROCKTON PUBLIC LIBRARY

Imagine the moon.
    What do you see?

Is she a peach,
    hanging ripe from a tree?
Is she a baby face,
    peeking from clouds,
here and there, and in and out?

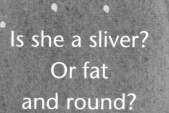

IMAGINE THE MOON

The moon is the earth's only satellite and measures 2,159 miles in diameter. The earth is a bit less than three times as large as the moon with a diameter of 7,917.5 miles.

The moon has barely any atmosphere or water. When space debris hits the moon, it leaves a crater. Without wind or rain to erode it, the mark of the crater is permanently etched in the surface of the moon.

The biggest crater on the moon is so big we don't even call it a crater. It's a basin! The Aitken Basin measures 2,500 kilometers (1,553.4 miles) across and is the largest, deepest, and oldest basin on the moon.

Is she a sliver?
Or fat
and round?

Close enough to touch
or high above the ground?

Imagine the moon,
how she waxes and wanes.
Imagine the moon,
each month, changing her name.

WOLF MOON (January)

Have you ever howled at the moon? The moon has inspired many songs. Beethoven's Piano Sonata No. 14 (also known as "Moonlight Sonata") sounds like moonlight shining on water. "O Mr. Moon (Please Shine Down on Me)" and "Shine On, Harvest Moon" are fun to sing around a campfire.

Astronomers will tell you that the whole universe sings. Radio telescopes detect the sounds of the stars. In 1964, two radio astronomers, Robert Wilson and Arno Penzias, first heard the sound of the universe being born 13.8 billion years ago through the discovery of Cosmic Microwave Background Radiation (CMB). Scientists call this "birthday song" the Big Bang.

In 2003 and again in 2013, inspired by a question from a fifth grader, John Cramer, a physicist at the University of Washington, created a soundtrack that simulated the Big Bang.

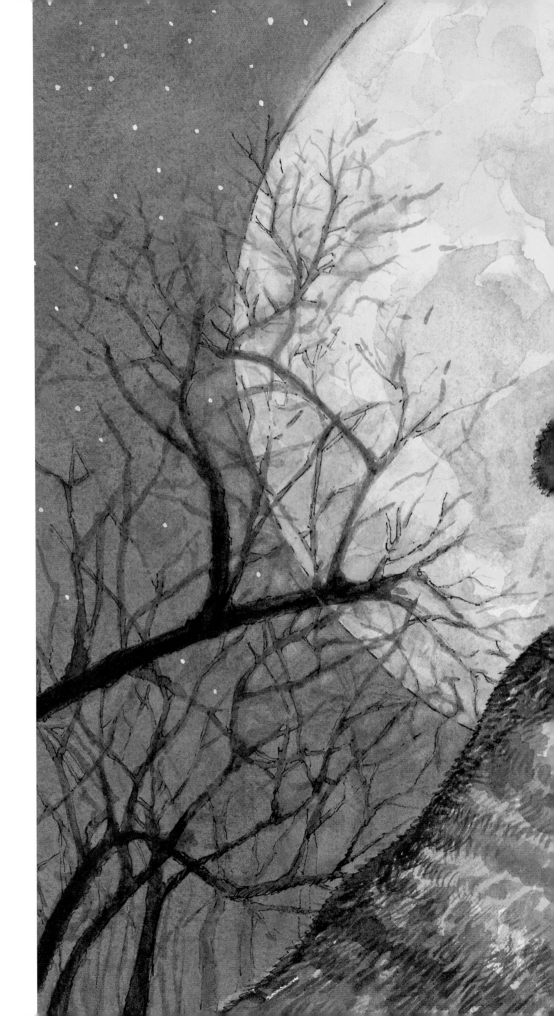

Wolf Moon
shines over January nights,
singing songs of shining lights.

Snow Moon

makes February bright,
cold, clear beams cutting the night.

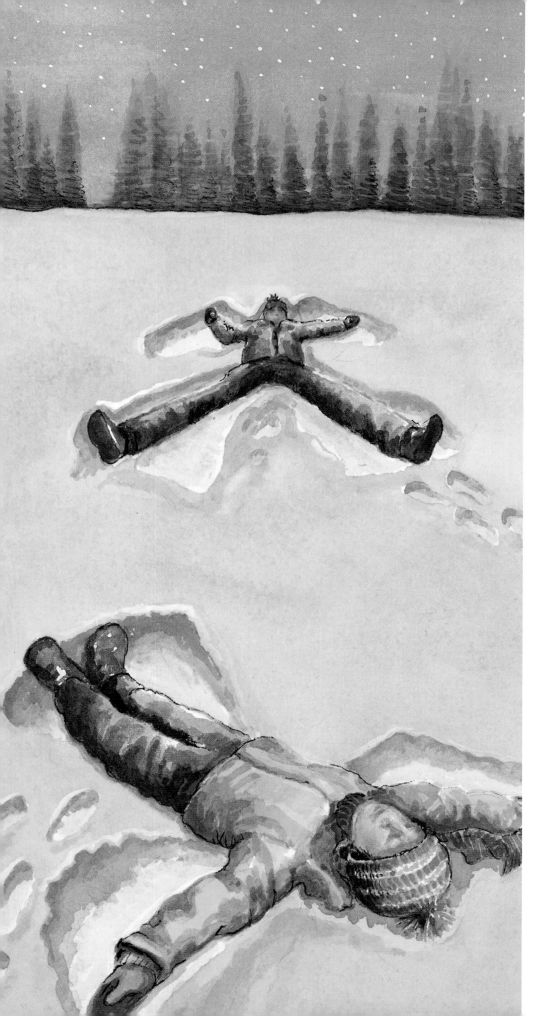

SNOW MOON (February)

Everyone loves to play with snow, even grownups. In 2011, Nova Scotia residents set a world record when 22,022 people, in 130 different locations, plopped down and wiggled their arms and legs to simultaneously sculpt 22,022 snow angels.

Washington State's Mount Rainier claims the heaviest snowfall ever recorded in the U.S. within one year's time: 102 feet of snow fell between February 19, 1971, and February 19, 1972. That is as high as a ten-story building!

Just as the white color of snow comes from reflected light off a snowflake's many-sided crystal of ice, the white "snowball" color of the moon is the result of reflected light from the sun bouncing off the lunar surface. The earth's gravity slows the moon's rotation so that, as it spins, we always see the same side of the moon facing us. Sunlight, striking the circling positions of the spinning earth and moon, makes shadows that form the shapes that the moon takes on during its lunar cycle.

Worm Moon
crawls high in greening March,
waking the fields with her light touch.

WORM MOON (March)

In winter, earthworms burrow as far as six feet down to escape frozen ground. There, they curl up tight, insulate themselves with slime, and hibernate. When spring comes and the soil thaws, they crawl to the surface, churning the soil with slime. Slime is good! High in nitrogen, slime feeds growing plants and binds the soil together to create good soil texture. Good quality soil, such as farm land, will have close to 1.75 million worms per acre.

Earthworms also form the basis of many food chains. They are a staple food for many types of birds, snakes, moles, hedgehogs, beetles, snails, slugs, and mammals such as raccoons, skunks, foxes, and bears. Charles Darwin thought that earthworms were just about the most important creatures on earth, writing, "It may be doubted if there are any other animals which have played such an important part in the history of the world as these lowly organized creatures."

PINK MOON (April)

The Pink Moon is so named because pink is the color of hope and rebirth, and April's full moon is the seasonal sign that the earth is awakening to new life. The Algonquin tribes, who populated an area from New England to the Great Lakes, noted wild ground phlox (also known as moss pink) heralding the arrival of spring and coloring the earth with brush strokes of pink. They—and the European colonists who arrived later—named the April moon after these flowers. On the other side of the world, at the base of Mount Fuji, the Japanese also celebrate the color of early blooming fields with the Shibazakura Festival, when 800,000 moss pink flowers blanket fields as far as the eye can see.

The earth's atmosphere, like a lens, filters moonlight, making it shine different colors. Although the moon rarely appears pink, it takes on a red color during a lunar eclipse and is commonly referred to as a blood moon.

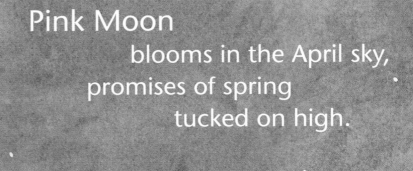

Pink Moon
blooms in the April sky,
promises of spring
tucked on high.

Flower Moon
sings a pretty May song
while frogs and peepers dance along.

FLOWER MOON (May)

Can you imagine the moon like a flower, slowly opening and closing throughout the month? There are, in fact, "moonflowers" that bloom at night. *Ipomoea alba* is a night-blooming morning glory known as "moonflower." You can easily start it from seed and grow it in your own garden. Its big white flowers open at night and resemble a full moon, but beware! It grows, and it grows, and it grows. Maybe it is trying to reach the moon!

We call the blossoming and fading appearance of the moon *waxing* and *waning*. Waxing is when the left side of the moon is dark and the lighted portion is slowly growing toward a full moon. Waning is when the right side of the moon is increasingly dark and the shadowed portion is moving toward a new moon.

Strawberry Moon
ripens on June's vine,
filled with the sweetness
of summertime.

STRAWBERRY MOON
(June)

Strawberries ripen in June, so this month's moon reminds us to go strawberry picking. In mythology, strawberries are associated with Freyja, the Norse goddess of love and the heart. Folklore says the sweetness of strawberries can encourage love, and June is a traditional time to get married. European folklore says that if you share a double strawberry with someone, you will fall in love with each other. Although strawberries will stain your lips and fingers red, their malic acid is a natural whitening agent for teeth and a common folk remedy for removing dental stains. So maybe it is true that red lips and white teeth make for sweet kisses!

California produces 88% of the strawberries in the U.S., more than 2.3 billion pounds a year. If all those strawberries were laid end to end, they would go around the world fifteen times!

Buck Moon
leaps across July
as shooting stars
flash across the sky.

BUCK MOON (July)

The buck, or male of the Cervidae family (including deer, elk, and moose), is distinguished by a crown of antlers that grow in response to the lengthening light of spring and drop in winter's darkness. By July, in summer's long light, a buck's horns peak in a large impressive crown.

Cervidae range in size from the tiny Andean pudu (16 inches tall and 22 pounds) to the moose (7 feet tall and 1,600 pounds). During the seasonal cycle, as the herds forage for food, they may migrate through a variety of habitats, including forest, grassland, and tundra. One of the marvelous sights of nature is the migration of reindeer in the Arctic, as great herds numbering in the tens of thousands move hundreds and sometimes thousands of miles.

Sturgeon Moon
　　swims against
　　　August's stream
　　　while dwindling days
　stretch into
　warm evenings.

STURGEON MOON
(August)

The Algonquin tribes near Lake Champlain and the Great Lakes named this moon because sturgeon were most easily caught in late summer. Sturgeon look like prehistoric fish. In fact, sturgeon fossils date back to the Triassic period some 200 million years ago.

The moon is about 4.5 billion years old, much older than any prehistoric life. About 100 million years after the birth of our solar system, a small planet nearly the size of Mars collided with the earth, punching debris into the planet's orbit. Slowly, gravity pulled all this rubble from the earth into a single sphere—the moon. Rocks brought back from the moon are the oldest that scientists have ever examined.

HARVEST MOON
(September)

All around the northern hemisphere, the Harvest Moon is a time of celebration as the fields offer their bounty. In English tradition, the harvest festival is held during the full moon closest to the autumn equinox. A thousand years ago, the Anglo-Saxon word for autumn was *haerfest,* from which we get *harvest,* a time of reaping and gathering. At *Haerfest,* everyone gathered to help harvest and celebrate abundance.

At this time of year, Jews around the world celebrate Succot, the Feast of the Tabernacles. Families gather to eat in a sukkah, a temporary dwelling decorated with autumn fruits and whose roof is open to the sky.

In China and Vietnam, families gather under the harvest moon and share round mooncakes as a symbol of completeness and connection. Lanterns are lit and sometimes launched into the sky. One game families play is to write riddles on the lanterns for others to answer. Here's a riddle: *How does the moon cut his hair?* Answer: *He eclipse it.*

Harvest Moon
is a lantern on September's fields,
lighting the fiddler as he clicks his heels.

Hunter's Moon

burns through October's chill,
a campfire glow with smoky tendrils.

HUNTER'S MOON
(October)

Artemis, the ancient Greek moon goddess, is a huntress, protector of the wildlands, and mistress of animals. Hunting and respect for the wild are linked values.

Prehistoric hunters, observing the natural world, tracked the passage of time by looking at the moon to follow the changing seasons. As long as 34,000 years ago, they carved bone, antler, and stone to create lightweight lunar calendars. In October, sunset and moonrise come close together, providing extended light for tracking herds of mammoths, bison, elk, or horses. The animals had fattened over the summer and were migrating by early fall. The Hunter's Moon signaled that the season had come to hunt and gather food for the coming winter.

To this day, even in areas where food is commercially available every day of the year, October ushers in hunting season across the United States.

Beaver Moon
builds a
November lair,
storing the light
of the dwindling year.

BEAVER MOON
(November)

The beaver is a builder, creating a cycle that echoes the cycle of earth and sky. Just as the moon has its waxing and waning cycle, just as the moon causes the cycles of the rising and falling tides, so a beaver dam creates a cycle. The beaver pond floods woodlands to create wetlands until aquatic plants take over and silt builds up. Then shrubs and other plants grow, and the area becomes a meadow. Eventually, bushes fill out to provide shade for tree seedlings until trees take over, creating woodlands and completing the cycle.

The Cold Moon
is December's fate.
Icicle beams greet winter's weight.

COLD MOON
(December)

As cold fills the longest nights of the year, the Cold Moon reaches its highest point in the northern sky. December marks the beginning of winter, a time to bundle up and take a walk under the clear moonlight. Even the moonbeams seem to cover the earth with ice.

With barely any atmosphere, the surface of the moon reaches extreme cold and hot. On the dark side of the moon, the temperature averages –298 degrees Fahrenheit, and when sunlight hits the side of the moon we see, the average temperature rises to +224 degrees Fahrenheit. When astronauts visit the moon, their spacesuits not only give them air to breath but also regulate their body temperature.

Once every month,
the moon grows full,
but a
Blue Moon
shines twice,
breaking this rule.

BLUE MOON
(Thirteenth Moon)

Have you heard the expression "once in a Blue Moon"? It refers to something that rarely happens. Because the lunar cycle averages 29.5 days, slightly shorter than a calendar month, approximately every thirty-three months, thirteen full moons occur in one year. In that case, one calendar month will have two full moons; the second one is called a Blue Moon.

An event that is rarer than a Blue Moon is a journey to the moon! Although people have talked and dreamed of such flights for thousands of years, only twelve men have actually walked on the moon. On July 20, 1969, Neil Armstrong was the first of these American astronauts. As he took the first step on the moon, he said, "That's one small step for a man, one giant leap for mankind." About twenty minutes later, Buzz Aldrin followed him. Michael Collins, the third member of this team, remained in orbit, piloting the command module.

Imagine the moon bringing sweet dreams,
tucking you in amidst the moonbeams.
The moon is never constant but will always be there,
the stuff that makes magic out of thin air.
Poets and pranksters, kids and kings,
imagine the moon, imagine and dream.